Traffic Tidal Wave

20 of the Best Known Ways to Get Traffic Online

Jim Stephens

Contents

Introduction

If you are getting into Internet marketing, it is quite certain that you must be finding different ways of attracting traffic to your business each time you do some research.

Remember that the strength is not in numbers here, it lies in the quality of your approach toward traffic generation.

So what are the best ways to attract traffic to your website?

Grab a mug of coffee, sit back in your cozy computer chair and read on. We present here the 20 best ways marketers use for traffic generation.

Traffic Tidal Wave Method # 1

Pay Per Click Services

Pay per click or PPC is a model in which you pay advertisers according to the number of clicks they can generate for your website. The concept is very simple. You use Google AdWords (http://adwords.google.com/) or another PPC software and become a member. Then you submit your URL to them which you want to promote. The PPC service will then find other website owners on the Internet that are interested in promoting your website URL. These are your affiliates. They will place your URL on their sites in the form of an advertisement and whenever any person clicks on them, you pay them.

There are other methods to pay out; PPC is not the only one. Many services also provide a Pay Per Sale model (PPS) where you pay out only when a sale has been done. There is also a Pay Per Lead model (PPL) where you pay out when the visitor takes some particular action such as providing their email id, which becomes a lead.

If you haven't tried out PPC yet, you are surely missing the number 1 traffic generation method which every Internet marketer worth their salt is using. It isn't quite difficult to get into this medium of promotion – you must start researching on it pronto.

The following is a list of some other PPC software applications that you can use instead of Google AdWords.

Yahoo! Campaign Optimization (http://searchmarketing.yahoo.com/)

MSN AdCenter (http://adcenter.microsoft.com/)

Omniture (http://www.omniture.com/)

Apex Reach (http://www.apexreach.com/)

Atlas Search (http://www.atlassolutions.com/services_search.aspx/)

KeywordMax (http://www.keywordmax.com/)

SearchRev (http://www.searchrev.com/)

SearchFeed (http://www.searchfeed.com/)

SearchIgnite (http://about.searchignite.com/)

♦ ♦ ♦

Traffic Tidal Wave Method # 2

SEO

Search engine optimization, abbreviated as SEO, has been a buzzword in the Internet marketing world for several years now. Basically it means making a website better searchable by the search engines. Marketers who are looking at optimizing their websites work with regards to one of three major search engines – Google, Yahoo! Or MSN – because all these three have different parameters for organizing their links.

Out of this Google is the most popular and most marketers wish that their rank – called as PageRank in Google parlance – improves. Since Google is a context based search engine (which means it ranks content-rich websites higher than others), marketers use the following methods for improving their PageRank on Google:-

→ They research on keywords and use them in their content. Google ranks websites based on the number of currently popular keywords that it contains.

→ Apart from keyword optimization, the overall content matters too. There must at least a 250 word content on a webpage for it to be considered by Google.

→ The content needs to be regularly updated too. Google is looking for content that provides value to the reader. Content that keeps changing is looked upon as dynamic content that the visitor would like.

Speaking in a broader sense, all methods of traffic generation are SEO methods. There's a reason behind this. Search engines like Google keep a watch on the popularity of websites. According to them, if a website is visited more, it contains good value. Hence, websites that generate traffic automatically end up with better stakes on the search engines.

We shall be learning many more SEO methods in the course of this eBook.

◆ ◆ ◆

Traffic Tidal Wave Method # 3

Blogging and Forum Posting

You surely know what blogs and forums are. Though blogs and forums are different from each other, there's one thing that's common between them. Both of them allow visitors to post comments on them. That is the reason why they become interactive tools for the marketers of today.

Many marketers are known to start blogs of their own and make a post about their industry or even about their own product. They then put the link of their business website in the post or below it (below is considered more dignified). Visitors read the post and may probably visit the link mentioned. Thus, blogging is a good method of traffic generation.

Now, it is not necessary for you to have your own blog to market through them. (Incidentally if you want to make your own blog, software such as Blogger, available at http://www.blogger.com/, and Wordpress, available at http://www.wordpress.com/ can help you.) You could even visit blogs and forums of other people that are active on the Internet and make your comment on them. Even these have the same result; you get people coming in through the promoted link.

Forums follow a similar principle, but here you have to follow threads. Check out Digital Point Forums (http://forums.digitalpoint.com/) to see how the system works. Here you can initiate a thread. Forums have a better approach than blogs because here you will find only people who are very serious in the industry. Thus, both blogs and forums can improve the amount of traffic that your website is getting if you do them correctly.

♦ ♦ ♦

Traffic Tidal Wave Method # 4

Article Submissions

Submitting articles for traffic generation is a method that has been around since the beginning of the concept of Internet marketing and it is still going great guns. The fact that websites like Google rank content-rich websites better is what consolidates its position. Article submission is definitely one of the best methods of SEO available in today's times.

The concept is simple – you write a keyword rich article and then you submit it on various article directories. You are given a bio box at the bottom of the article where you can put in your and your business' name, with the link of the website that you want to promote. You can also put in a brief description about yourself in this box.

When a person stumbles upon on your website – the chances of which are high because you will be keyword optimizing your article – there is a likelihood that they will like your article and will then click on the link to get more information. This is how you get your traffic through article marketing.

Marketers use various article directories, most of which are free. The following is a list of some very good article marketing directories:-

Ezine Articles (http://www.ezinearticles.com/)

iSnare (http://www.isnare.com/)

Go Articles (http://www.goarticles.com/)

Articles Base (http://www.articlesbase.com/)

Article City (http://www.articlecity.com/)

Article Alley (http://www.articlealley.com/)

Buzzle (http://www.buzzle.com/)

By saying good we mean article directories that are ranked well by the search engines. You can even submit the same article on several of these directories, which is what many marketers do. However, you must make sure that you keep the same author name, or it could count as plagiarism. The best way, of course, is to make a little variation in the articles when submitting to each directory so that it looks different. You could even do that with software known as content spinning software. This software can produce variations of an article so that they are not rapped on the knuckles by search engines for duplication. However, since the quality of spun articles is not good, you will need to do some manual editing once they are spun.

The following are two popular content spinning software applications that some top Internet marketers use:-

Content Spinner (http://www.contentspinner.com/)

Content Spooler (http://www.contentspooler.com/)

◆ ◆ ◆

Traffic Tidal Wave Method # 5

Traffic Exchange Programs

Traffic exchange programs are places where you can submit your website link. This is a membership place. All members will submit their own links. The idea is to get together and promote each other's links as though this is a giant affiliate program, where every website owner is an affiliate of the other.

The direct benefit is that there is a whole army of people promoting your website and not just you, which means that you get some stupendous publicity. Your website link jumps up several notches on the search engine ranking and the Alexa rankings because of the great publicity that this generates. In other words, you get a breathtaking amount of traffic.

There are free traffic exchange programs where you can submit the link of your website for free, only in exchange for promoting other website links. However, there is another mode at work here too. You can click on the links of other websites, becoming traffic for them, which gives you points. When you get a particular number of points, you can submit your website link too.

You might ask how this is beneficial to the website submitters since you have clicked on the links without any intention of buying anything. Actually, it still works, because you are trafficking the site. This makes the search engine think that the website is popular and it gives the website a better rank. Your clicks have propelled the website to a higher position on the search engine results.

The following are some popular traffic exchange sites:-

Traffic G (http://www.trafficg.com/)

Web Traffic Genie (http://www.webtrafficgenie.com/)

Easy Hits 4 U (http://www.easyhits4u.com/)

Click Thru (http://www.clickthru.com/)

Traffic Swarm (http://www.trafficswarm.com/)

Link Referral (http://www.linkreferral.com/)

◆ ◆ ◆

Traffic Tidal Wave Method # 6

Directory Submission

Directory submission is another SEO method that holds a promise of good traffic. It is very similar to the previously mentioned traffic exchange programs and in fact most marketers consider them to be exactly the same. But there are differences here in which marketers can submit their websites. The website links are not randomly accepted by the directories, but they have to fulfill certain qualifications, which might be following a particular niche. The websites are ranked by the directory on the basis of the value that they can provide to a potential visitor.

The rest of the concept is the same. As more and more people visit these links, the website begins ranking better. We say that the website gets better search engine optimized. Hence, this is a method that you should not avoid for generating traffic.

The task that takes the highest amount of time here is the submission itself. Though there are automatic submission services available, most marketers still use the manual submission route because that spells quality. Freelancers are employed most times for getting these submissions done so that the marketers can focus on their other more important tasks.

There are two main types of directory submission services provided. One of these is specific to the kinds of keywords that are used. Keyword optimization becomes important so that the website link gets accepted by the directory. The other method is a normal directory submission. Here back links are provided so that the websites can be visited. Both kinds of directories are very popular with Internet marketers.

The following are some directory submission services that you can use:-

Best Web Directories (http://www.best-web-directories.com/)

AboutUs.org (http://www.aboutus.org/)

Yahoo! Directory (http://dir.yahoo.com/)

The following are some special niche directories:-

For the business niche – Business.com (http://www.business.com/)

For the biography niche – Biographicon (http://www.biographicon.com/)

◆ ◆ ◆

Traffic Tidal Wave Method # 7

Link Exchange Programs

Link exchange programs are just what their names indicate. Website owners promote each other's links on their sites. These are similar to traffic exchange programs in that many people come together to promote each other's businesses. But the difference lies in the way this promotion is done. In traffic exchange programs, the link promotion is done on a separate website directory. However, in link exchange programs, the promotion is done on the websites of the participants themselves.

Link exchange is done through text as well as banners. The people who want to promote their sites make their links available in the form of HTML codes or banners. These are then picked up by other webmasters and promoted on their own sites.

The main intention is, of course, to get as much visibility as possible. When more people begin clicking on the ads, the SEO of the link automatically increases and still more people come in. Like many other SEO methods, implementing a suitable link exchange program helps you to get more eyeballs on your website.

But there is a distaff side of link exchange that you have to think of. You need to promote your website link only on websites that are equal to or greater in popularity than yours. Submitting to a low ranking website will do nothing to your PageRank. Similarly, you should not accept sites that are very low in status than yours. This will adversely affect your own PageRank.

You can get free websites for link submission as well. For this you will need to contact the website owner directly. Use a service such as WhoIS to know who the owner of a particular website is and their email contact so that you can communicate with them directly. You can find details about any webmaster of any website using WhoIS which you can obtain from http://ping.eu.

Link exchange is a very good method of bringing in traffic to your website; however, if you are looking for targeted traffic – i.e. traffic that will be really interested in buying your products – you will need to look harder and use some other methods in conjunction with this.

◆ ◆ ◆

Traffic Exchange Method # 8

Email Marketing

Email marketing is based on lead generation. Leads are people who have done some activity on your website or on an affiliate website – such as downloading an eBook or adding themselves to an opt-in list or subscribing to a newsletter, etc. – and have given their email id in the process. The email id is called as the lead. The collection of all these people is known as the list.

The actual process of email marketing involves sending informative content through email to these people on your list. The emails have to be content-rich, providing them something of value and very subtly nudging them to perform some further action, such as visit your website for an offer or a free gift. Though the eventual intention is selling the product, it is not done blatantly in email marketing.

Email marketing brings in a lesser flow of traffic than other methods generate. Despite that, marketers use this method prominently. The main reason for that lies in the fact that the low traffic brought by this method is all targeted traffic. The people who have opted in to become part of your list are people who are interested in your list. It is very easy to get them to convert. This is the method they refer to when they say – "Get the customers to come to you; don't go to them yourself."

But, the success of this method lies in your email. You have to take care that you provide something of immense value that these people can use. These can be:-

→ Some latest news about the industry

→ An easier way to do ordinary things related to the niche

→ A set of tips, pointers or guidelines

→ A short but effective how-to guide

→ Directions for getting freebies and discounted offers within the niche

→ Success stories of other people

→ Motivational material

... and so on. People are looking for such information on the Internet anyway. When you send this directly to them in their inbox, your credibility increases. Not only do you get traffic, but you also get repeated traffic and conversions.

♦ ♦ ♦

Traffic Exchange Method # 9

Social Networking Sites

Social networking has become immensely popular in today's times. Everyone from freckle-faced teenagers to octogenarians is using these sites and, in fact, they are spending a lot of time on them. As a marketer, you just cannot avoid the potential of these websites in making your site highly-trafficked.

One reason why social networking works as a method of traffic generation is that you can find people with various interests here, and most of them make their interests known through their profiles. Many social networking websites are searchable through meta tags, which are nothing but specialized keywords. Hence, if you have a business of selling a gardening product, you could easily put 'gardening' in the search bar of a social networking site and very soon a list of all the people who have listed gardening as a hobby in their public profiles will show up. Then you can send a bulk email to all these people speaking about your product and can even give them your business link to visit.

Do you realize what is happening here? You are marketing directly to people who are interested in gardening, which increases your traffic conversion rate manifold.

The best thing about social networking is that you don't have to go anywhere to build your list. You have it right there on the site. However, this also brings in competition. But, if your product does spell good quality and people are impressed by the content you provide them, you will stand out eventually.

Social marketing is a fast – almost instantaneous – method of getting traffic. People usually constantly monitor their social networking profiles. As soon as they get the email verification from you, they will want to visit the site and check out. This is your 'make or break' moment. You have to make sure your emails are right.

The following are three of the most popular social networking sites that Internet marketers use. Do you have profiles on them already?

Facebook (http://www.facebook.com/)

MySpace (http://www.myspace.com/)

Twitter (http://www.twitter.com/)

This is not the end. There are various niches here such as video sharing sites, photo sharing sites and several others like that which belong to a special niche of services. We will speak about them later in this eBook.

♦ ♦ ♦

Traffic Tidal Wave Method # 10

Video Sharing

Video sharing has becomes a much formidable method of traffic generation especially after the unbelievable popularity of YouTube. (http://www.youtube.com/). Today, there are several other wannabes that are in the YouTube mould, but for a marketer, video sharing has become synonymous with YouTube marketing.

The concept is simple again. You make an interesting video about some interesting aspect about your product and then post it on YouTube. With its millions of viewers per month, you can be sure that your video will be watched several times. If your video is good, you can draw visitors from your video to your website directly.

YouTube is built for marketers. It has a unique feature in which you can insert a website link into the video itself and make it clickable. Since the viewer doesn't have to undergo the hassle of seeing and typing the email address, you can be assured to getting more visitors. Also, you can improve the prospects of your video through content. YouTube allows meta tag descriptions, which means great SEO and also has content such as headlines which again you can spruce up for SEO. You must also note that YouTube is a Google subsidiary and hence it uses the amazing Google search engine.

Another thing that you must note is that YouTube is also a social networking site. You can make your account there and comment on videos and stuff. This means people get to talking about your video and the product shown therein. This leads to another awesome aspect of traffic generation, known as viral marketing.

◆ ◆ ◆

Traffic Tidal Wave Method # 11

Podcasting

Despite the fact that podcasting has been around for some time now, not many marketers are using it yet. Due to that reason, there is still the newness factor associated with it, which works to your advantage actually. This is still a new age technology which can bring a lot of targeted traffic to your door if you would let them in. Here is a brief look into how podcasting works.

Basically, podcasting is like having a radio channel of your own on the Internet. You do not have to bow down to any rules and regulations because none apply. You simply have your audio content which you are beaming to a lot of people on the Internet. These people are your audience. They have, in fact, asked to be marketed. They want to know about your products. When you podcast to them, there is a very high chance that these people will convert to being your visitors.

So why are these people hot traffic for you? The reason behind that is that podcasting works only for people who have subscribed to your RSS feeds. When you put up an audio segment, those audio files automatically get downloaded to the audio devices of the people who have subscribed to the feeds.

You need special software to create a podcast. This software is simply known as podcasting software or a podcasting mixer. Basically it is a tool that converts an audio file into a file into a digital file that can be downloaded over the Internet. The following is a list of two of the most popular podcasting software:-

Feed for All (http://www.feedforall.com/)

Podcast Studio (http://thepodcaststudio.com/)

Using podcasting sets you apart from the usual breed of Internet marketers. This is certainly a method that you need to seriously consider to improve your prospects.

♦ ♦ ♦

Traffic Tidal Wave Method # 12

Viral Marketing

Viral marketing is not just an Internet-based concept; it applies to the real world also. Fundamentally, viral marketing happens when someone who has used a product speaks about it favorably to another person. If you watch a movie and recommend it to your friend, you are virally marketing the movie. On the Internet, if you post a favorable comment about a product or a service, you are virally marketing it. In fact, on the Internet even if you criticize a product, you are virally marketing it. There's a reason behind that. Whatever your comment is, positive or negative, it does one thing – it increases the recall value of the product. People begin to identify the brand better. The product becomes more searchable over the Internet. Hence, viral marketing always works.

All social networking sites are avenues for virally marketing products. Your blogs are places where your product gets virally marketed. This also happens on forums and video and photo sharing sites. Your articles are tools of viral marketing too. So, you see that viral marketing is not an isolated method. It is, in fact, an umbrella term for the various marketing practices you employ.

Viral marketing works because it tells potential buyers about the product so that they begin thinking seriously about buying the product. It improves the recall value of a product and makes it more visible. On the Internet, a product that is visible is a hit.

◆ ◆ ◆

Traffic Tidal Wave Method # 13

Giving Away

Give, and you shall receive. Now, where have we heard this before?

Whether this adage works in all aspects of life or not is a matter of personal opinion, but on the Internet it always works. When you give something away, it helps in bringing in better prospects to your online business.

But, what can you give away? It is highly important that your giveaway is something or value. It should be something that a receiver would cherish, because this is what adds to your credibility as a service provider.

You might be having a question in your mind right now – how does a giveaway help in bringing traffic or business to your website?

This happens through lead capture methods. When you give something away, you put a link where people can download the product from. This link takes them through a lead capture page, also known as a squeeze page. Here they are asked to opt in with their email id so that they can get more such freebies in future. Assurances are made to the effect that their email id won't be sold over to anyone else and that spam won't be sent to them. People usually give their links because they know they will be getting something valuable for free. When you get these leads, you can market them through other ways such as email marketing.

So, what are the things that you can give away? Even giveaways undergo surges and ebbs in their popularity on the Internet. Currently, the best things to give away include the following:-

→ eBooks

→ Newsletter Subscriptions

→ Free Offers on Products from Partner Sites

→ Informative Listings

♦ ♦ ♦

Traffic Tidal Wave Method # 14

Yahoo! Answers

Yahoo! Answers (http://answers.yahoo.com/) is a place where people ask questions and other people answer them. In return they get points. The points that they get can be used for asking more questions; they have no real world value. However, this is an amazing way to get your queries answered, because you are mostly asking experts to help you out with things that you don't know.

This is also a great place for marketers because they can flaunt their knowledge. If someone asks a question pertaining to your line of business, you can answer them and improve your credibility. You also get business exposure, which is the most important thing, because you can post your business link in the answer you provide.

If you have a Yahoo! account already, you can use the same for your Yahoo! Answers campaign. You have to merely search for questions (which you can do with keywords) and then post your replies on them.

Make sure that your replies sound like an expert's view on the subject. This is a great way of convincing people about your expertise; don't let it pass by.

◆ ◆ ◆

Traffic Tidal Wave Method # 15

Squidoo

Though Squidoo marketing is a very new concept over the Internet, people have warmed to it pretty quickly, because of the various benefits that it has. The novelty factor is one of the prime benefits because not many marketers are using Squidoo yet and hence competition through this method is low. There's also the point that Squidoo has got an amazing rank on Google already. If you have a Squidoo page, or a Squidoo lens as they call it, the chances of it getting ranked well are high.

Squidoo (http://www.squidoo.com/) is basically a website where you can put your own content and promote your product or service. The page you create is called as a Squidoo lens. You post content here, with your website link and then wait for the people to come to you.

Why does Squidoo work? For many reasons actually, but one of the reasons is that it relies on content more than anything else. Various other methods have become popular for traffic generation and then have fizzled out, but the novelty with Squidoo is that it goes back to the past when content marketing was king. It still is, and that is amply shown by the popularity of Squidoo in bringing traffic.

Of course, the general content rules apply. Write great informative content and consolidate it by using great keywords.

◆ ◆ ◆

Traffic Tidal Wave Method # 17

USFreeAds

A lot of Internet marketers speak very favorably about USFreeAds (http://www.usfreeads.com/) and not without reason. This is a classified ads site that marketers use to drive traffic to their website. The site is used for promoting almost any kind of product. You create an HTML code for your ad and post it on the site from where it gets promoted. This is where the site brings the visitors from.

You will need to become a member on USFreeAds; it is not a free service. In order to become a member, there are three different methods. There is a gold membership that costs $10 a year and a premium membership that costs that amount a month. The third method is a free membership but that is very restrictive in the way you can generate traffic through it.

The ad is no different from other ads that you create around the Internet. Even here you make a headline and tag the ad so that the search engines find and rank it. There is also a content part in the ad where you put the main body of the ad.

One of the reasons why USFreeAds is great for generating traffic is that the ads that are created on this never expire. Also, the website is held in high esteem by Google, often shooting the ads to number one position in a short time.

♦ ♦ ♦

Traffic Tidal Wave Method # 17

Craigslist

Craigslist (http://www.craigslist.com/) is a highly reputed classified ads site which is a formidable marketing tool because it can bring in a huge volume of traffic. Today, Craigslist is widely known as the most popular advertising website known to humans. It is a city specific classifieds search, but it has a huge approach – at current standing, Craigslist ads are specific to more than 450 cities and new cities are constantly added. There are about 7 billion page views on Craigslist every month and about 20 million people visit the sites advertised on Craigslist every month. All this makes it very easy to see why Craigslist is one the most favored marketing tools.

When you make a Craigslist ad, most of the same rules apply as they do for other ad websites. You have to make sure that the headline is catchy, you have good meta tags defined, words are few and to the point, etc. With Craigslist you can build a back link to your main website and you can use a Do Follow tag. When you link the ad to your main website, you have to provide an anchor text. The anchor text is selected after careful consideration and is very much relevant to the ad website.

Google Analytics (http://analytics.google.com/) is an important tool that you can use in conjunction with Craigslist. It helps you know where your traffic is coming from. Once you know which your traffic hotspots are, you could exclude the ads that are not bringing in a good amount of traffic and focus on those that do.

Posting ads on Craigslist does not just help in making your website visible on the Internet; it also helps in improving its SEO. That is because as more people begin to click on your ad, your popularity on the Internet increases.

Craigslist is one of the best things that a marketer can do; you must surely not miss out on this one.

♦ ♦ ♦

Traffic Tidal Wave Method # 18

Digg

Digg (http://www.digg.com/) is a social networking website with a difference. The main hero here is the content, which are routine articles. Digg is a site where people can find things that they like and then recommend them to other people. These people generally promote things that they think their friends or contacts would like. If you think about it, Digg can be exploited to the hilt if you have great content that you are sure people will be talking about.

There is an internal ranking system on Digg. The higher the number of times your content is dugg, the greater is its popularity and the better are the chances that it will make the front page of Digg. The system is to put up your content and then wait for 24 hours to see how many votes it gets. This is the decider for it to be displayed on the main page or not.

The amount of popularity that Digg can bring about for your website is astounding. Getting a jump of about 10,000 to 15,000 visitors is quite natural, but there are people who have got as many as 200,000 extra visitors through Digg.

The content that you put up on Digg is in the form of an article. The article should be something that people like to read about. Some of the best things that you can put up on Digg include:-

→ Breaking News

→ How-to Guides

→ Informative Lists

→ Stories

→ Facts and Figures

...and such. You could write anything as long as it is relevant to your industry and you are sure that people will like to read about it.

Once they do, you are in the reckoning. People will digg what you have written, which will make it popular to others and you will gain better visibility.

♦ ♦ ♦

Traffic Tidal Wave Method # 19

StumbleUpon

StumbleUpon (http://www.stumbleupon.com/) is one more in the league of social bookmarking sites that intrepid Internet marketers cannot afford to ignore. This is a site where you can make people stumble upon your blog, regardless of whether they are consciously looking forward to it or not.

The way to begin with StumbleUpon is to first have a blog that is rich in content and information. It is great if the blog is set within a particular niche. Once the blog is ready, StumbleUpon is used on it. This is in the form of a toolbar that you download and install from their website.

Once the StumbleUpon toolbar has been installed on the blog, people will begin rating your blog on it. The higher the rating it gets, the better are your chances of getting noticed on the Internet.

StumbleUpon is very close in outlook to Digg, but while Digg is broader in nature, catering to all sectors of society, StumbleUpon is mainly used by niche marketers.

♦ ♦ ♦

Traffic Tidal Wave Method # 20

Social Bookmarking

Social bookmarking is when someone comes across a website and then bookmarks it for future reference. In the world that we live in, people don't just want to keep what they like from others. In fact, the sooner a website is added as a bookmark, the better it is because that means a lot more visitors will come to your website.

Digg and StumbleUpon are social bookmarking sites, but differences abound in both of them. Digg is mainly for the general audience, who want o know about various things. StumbleUpon helps to define niches so that a whirlpool of targeted traffic can visit your Internet offering.

The world that we live in is the world of Web 2.0. People have got all the options needed to find out about products on the Internet before they decide to purchase it. This is where social bookmarking comes in handy. If people genuinely like a product, they will surely recommend it to others.

◆ ◆ ◆

Conclusion

So now you have the 20 most important Internet marketing, you are on the way to becoming an unstoppable Internet marketer.

To your success!

www.ingramcontent.com/pod-product-compliance
Lightning Source LLC
Chambersburg PA
CBHW070905070326
40690CB00009B/2003